The Coast of Almería

Editorial Everest would like to thank you for purchasing this book. It has been created by an extensive and complete publishing team made up of photographers, illustrators and authors specialised in the field of tourism, together with our modern cartography department. Everest guarantees that the contents of this work were completely up to date at the time of going to press, and we would like to invite you to send us any information that helps us to improve our publications, so that we may always offer QUALITY TOURISM.

QUALITY
TOURISM
WITH
EVEREST

Please send your comments to:
Editorial Everest. Dpto. de Turismo
Apartado 339 – 24080 León (Spain)
Or e-mail them to us at turismo@everest.es

Editorial management: Raquel López Varela

Editorial coordination: Eva María Fernández Álvarez and Esteban González

Text: José Luis Laynez Bretones

Photographs: Juan José Pascual, Photobox and Archivo Everest

Diagrams: José Manuel Núñez

Cover design: Alfredo Anievas

Digital image processing: David Aller

Cartography: © Everest

Translated by: Traductores e Intérpretes EURO:TEXT, S. L. (Alayna Keller)

© EDITORIAL EVEREST, S. A.
Carretera León - La Coruña, km 5 - LEÓN
ISBN: 84-241-0152-9
Legal deposit: LE. 745 - 2001
Printed in Spain

EDITORIAL EVERGRÁFICAS, S. L.
Carretera León - La Coruña, km 5
LEÓN (Spain)

Cabo de Gata Park. The coast of Rodalquilar.

Almería has been blessed by nature with no less than 175 kilometres of shoreline. In all fairness, it must be said that not every foot of that shoreline is beaches and coves with billows of fine sand; sometimes the sea smashes straight into the cliffs or a jumble of boulders blocks all easy routes to the shore. But wait, let's not get too dramatic either. That's generally not the way it is on the Almería coast. Usually a stroll around any coastal village will eventually find broad beaches with fine sand and warm waters or cosy coves where we can have a private swim.

What's more, Almería isn't one of those sections of the coast that enjoyed their short-lived tourist boom years ago and now wonder where all the life and the money have gone. In Almería we have the last virgin Mediterranean beaches, and even in the most developed areas building and services never encroach upon the areas set aside for bathing. Almería is not one of those places where coach after coach of tourists swarm in until the beach looks more like an anthill than a bathing spot. Our beaches still have that comfortable family feeling. We almost all know one another and enjoy a friendly chat before and after a relaxing swim, a comforting walk and a refreshing glass of beer with fresh-caught sardines at the nearest beachfront stall.

If you take a survey of Almería's beaches from west to east, you may be pleasantly surprised by the villages, dependencies, townships, housing estates and nature reserves you will find there. And fortunately a good number of them are not too well known and the roads leading to them are sometimes not the best. When cities and towns are right on the coast we can readily reach their beaches, but often the road doesn't stick to the coast, so more than half the shore is challenging to get to. On this journey, if you'll accompany me, we are going to take our time getting to know the beaches of my Almería, starting at Granada (the beaches by Adra) and working our way up to where Andalusia bumps against Murcia (the beaches by Pulpí).

A trip from the westernmost edge of the province would start at **Adra,** which is roughly 50 kilometres from the regional capital of Almería. Adra, originally named *Abdera,* was founded by the Phoenicians. The town has always kept its arms open to the sea; the first fishing port in the entire province was built in Adra. It is the natural marine outlet for the La Alpujarra region of Spain, and when the last Moorish king of Spain, Boabdil, left his kingdom forever he sailed from Adra. The coast road leads us across the Albufera coastal lagoon to the municipal district of **El Ejido.** There we will find beaches like Balerma, a charming Mediterranean-style township; Guardias Viejas, watched over by an impressive castle; the modern and luxurious Urbanización Almerimar housing estate; and the Punta Entinas-Sabinar Natural Space that El Ejido shares with the neighbouring district of Roquetas de Mar.

Roquetas de Mar is the biggest tourist site in the province, as you might gather from its abundant supply of hotels. By the way, the local housing estate, Urbanización Roquetas de Mar, is one of the finest complexes the Mediterranean has to offer. After Roquetas we come to **Aguadulce,** which is officially a township dependent on Roquetas de Mar and also has a well-equipped housing estate, the oldest in the province, with its own marina. About ten kilometres up a lovely road that practically hangs from the cliff tops is the capital city of Almería, known to the Romans as *Urci* and to the Moslems as *Al Mariya.* Following the coast we zip right through Almería and on to one of the least crowded beaches on the coast, La Universidad. The beaches of Costacabana and Retamar lie in a gorgeous bay that spikes out at the cape, Cabo de Gata, at the tip of one of the province's natural gems, the **Cabo de Gata Natural Park.** Virgin beaches with hardly a building or other sign of man to upset the landscape bear names with suggestive overtones: Cabo de Gata is Cat Cove; Los Genoveses, the Genovese; la Isleta del Moro, the Moor's Islet; Las Negras means "the Black Ones;" San José sounds tropical; and Los Escullos and Mónsul are so musical. Here the road ends, but the coast goes on. On foot we can continue through coves of exquisite lonely beauty, such as the Cala de San Pedro, which has a freshwater spring fit to drink from and the remains of an old Nasrid castle.

The beach at Mónsul.

View of the port of Almería with the Alcazaba rising behind it.

By the time we reach the municipal district of **Carboneras,** at about Aguamarga, the asphalt reappears in the midst of a breathtaking landscape with oasis-like plant life. Next we reach **Mojácar,** a hamlet that glows with light, whitewashed walls and mystery. Mojácar's unmistakable Arab charm has elicited an excellent tourist response at its beaches, where we can find the province's only Parador de Turismo from the state-operated chain of inns. The people who live year-round at the coast, however, prefer to sunbathe at **Garrucha,** a perfect blend of old fishing village tradition and modern tourist development. Garrucha is rumoured to have the tastiest fish on the entire coast.

The road here clings to the coast and runs through the municipal districts of **Vera** and **Cuevas de Almanzora.** The actual villages are rather stately, set back a few kilometres from their respective beaches. The coast along here is speckled with coves, cliffs, old mining settlements and little half-finished housing estates like Puerto Rey, Villaricos, Palomares and El Pozo del Esparto. San Juan de los Terreros, at the edge of Almería and Andalusia in the municipal district of **Pulpí,** about 120 kilometres from the capital, is where our journey ends.

Torre del Pirulí, between Cala Bordonales and Macenas. ▶

Panoramic view of the port at Adra.

THE WESTERN BEACHES

The Beaches at Adra

The beaches at Adra are the westernmost beaches of our province and probably the first beaches to be used as such. And since Adra was founded by the Phoenicians, that makes it the oldest town on the Almería coast. The Greek geographer Strabo wrote in the first century B.C., "Abdera is the work of Phoenicians, the first land they trod when they were sent to Iberia by the voice of the oracle." It seems the town's original location was where the town of **La Alquería** now sits, about three kilometres inland; apparently the sea must have reached that far back then. As the river delta crept outward, the town had to move with it to remain in contact with the sea.

The traditional mainstays of Adra's economy are fishing, farming and mining. In fact Adra built itself the province's first port in 1911, although rather than facilitating the fishing trade the port was installed by imperative of the town's lead-smelting industry. Just a handful of tottering late nineteenth-century chimneys remain from Adra's once busy smelting furnaces.

Other industries soon followed suit. Adra used to have some very important sugar refineries fuelled by the sugarcane plantations that occupied the fertile plain. We can still see the chimneystacks and other remains of the Santa Julia refinery, though it is now completely abandoned, as are the salting and fish and vegetable canning factories. Adra did its best to support the local industrial revolution but unfortunately the enthusiasm did not spread to other nearby towns and eventually petered out.

At right, Torre del Perdigón.

Below, Torre de Guainos, in Adra.

Two statues occupying centric locations in the town give us a hint at the traditional occupations here in Adra: One is a statue to the farmer and stands under an arch at the entrance to the Plaza de San Sebastián, and the other, a statue to the fisherman, is located of course at the fishing port. Adra has, as we said, the oldest port in the province, and also the port with the highest annual catch. Fishing boats are still to be seen chugging out to sea with the first shadows of evening and returning at dawn. And the fish they bring is auctioned off as soon as it hits the docks in an atmosphere of noisy cheer.

Before we leave **Adra,** let me just point you toward a couple of visits you ought to make: One to the parish church, where you will find a Baroque carving of Christ, *el Cristo de la Expiración,* and the town patron, Virgin Mary of the Sea, commissioned by the seamen's guild; and the other to the nearby Albufera, a beautiful natural space whose wide marshes are home to hibernating anatides, coots, Spanish pond turtles and great numbers of reptiles and fish. In spring mallards, red-crested pochards, little grebes, storks and bitterns nest here. Ah! And if you can, some year try to catch the seagoing procession that Adra celebrates in September during the festivals in honour of its patron saint. They load the Virgin Mary on a boat and the entire local fleet escorts her up and down the beaches of Adra, sounding horns all the while. This is always quite a colourful event and a real people magnet.

Below, the Adra lighthouse.

Beaches at Adra. ▶

Above, the lagoon or Albufera in Adra.

◄ *Previous two pages, view of Adra.*

Below, Adra at festival time.

The Beaches at El Ejido

Though it mayn't seem so, the municipal district of **Berja** also has a toe in the water, the township of Balanegra. **Balanegra** is a lovely seaside village that may be changing gradually under the influence of tourism but hasn't lost a smidgen of its traditional family charm. It has a wide (2,640-metre) beach of coarse black sand.

Crossing over into the municipal district of El Ejido, the first town we hit along our way is **Balerma,** a near twin to Balanegra. Balerma is a seagoing village but it has of late been listening to the siren song of tourism, though it hasn't yet jumped overboard, fortunately. Next we come to **Guardias Viejas,** a township on the site of some old hot springs, once used for bathing but now abandoned, in the shadow of the local castle. The castle has been restored just recently, and a fine job they have done too, inside and out, with exhibitions, gardens and special night-time lighting. I hope you'll pay a call.

The next place the coastal road takes us is Urbanización **Almerimar,** a modern and unexpectedly green housing estate, quite the oasis in the arid land we've been travelling. This is because of Almerimar's carefully tended gardens and its wonderful eighteen hole golf course designed personally by Gary Player. Even if you're not especially keen on the game your eyes will enjoy resting on this emerald carpet and the luxurious hotel nearby surrounded by 2,500 square metres of pampered gardens and set off by a wonderful swimming pool.

Playa de Balanegra, in Berja.

El Ejido Church.

El Ejido Town Hall.

Aerial view of El Ejido, a quilt of greenhouses. ▶

Castillo de Guardas Viejas.

Below, the beach at Balerma.

Almerimar marina.

Almerimar also has a charming marina with 1,000 berths for crafts up to 60 metres long. The modern stone-faced building there is the Club Náutico, which organises prestigious national regattas. Pubs, restaurants and all kinds of shops line the surrounding colonnades. And on the anecdotal side, you might be interested to know that several ex-players for the Real Madrid football team have homes in Almerimar, where they stayed the night before their game against A. D. Almería (when Almería was in the first division of the Spanish league). You'll recognise the neighbourhood when you see it because of its name, Villa Merengue (supporters of the Real Madrid are nicknamed *merengues).*

After we leave Almerimar a narrow winding little road takes us into the **Punta Entinas y Punta Sabinar Nature Reserve** straddling the municipal districts of El Ejido and Roquetas de Mar. Punta Entinas y Punta Sabinar is an officially catalogued *natural space* and it is indeed beautiful as well as ecologically valuable. The reserve stretches up and down the coast, nearly a kilometre wide and about 16 kilometres long, and it covers 1,960 hectares. In it we can find little ponds where hundreds of waterfowl take refuge from May to November including coots, flamingos, red-crested and other pochards, northern shovellers, grey herons, avocets, gulls and various species of charadriiforms. The Punta Entinas Lighthouse is a great place to go for the view; from the top you can see vast stretches of the sea. Yes, it's worth all the stairs. And if you fish, whether with rod and reel or face mask and snorkel, you will find a real paradise here. On the sea bed you are just as likely to see groupers and sargos as you are to stumble across Phoenician or Greek amphorae.

Urbanización Almerimar, with its 18-hole golf course.

Two aerial views of Almerimar, in El Ejido. ▶

Above, wild birds in the Roquetas salt marsh.

Below, the beach at Punta Sabinar.

Above, Punta Entinas, El Ejido.

Below, salt marsh in Roquetas.

Playa de Roquetas.

The Beaches at Roquetas de Mar

Following the coastline, we will experience a startlingly brusque change of scenery. We know Almería is a land of contrasts, but will we ever get used to it? You see, we have just reached the cosmopolitan housing estate of Urbanización **Roquetas,** just two kilometres from the town of Roquetas. Three quarters of the province's hotel accommodations are right here. A walk along its avenues and streets plunges us into a world apart from the places we have been visiting until now: shops of every kind, ice cream parlours, coffee houses, seafood eateries, pizza parlours, hamburger joints, fish and chip shops, bakeries, restaurants serving Spanish food, German food, French food and even Oriental food line the arcaded sidewalks of Urbanización Roquetas.

The beaches here are wide, clean and equipped with all the amenities. In fact, there are three beaches, *Playa Serena, La Romanilla* and *Roquetas.* All are plentifully stocked with stands where you can refresh yourself with a pint and a nice snack of fresh roast fish. You can also seize the opportunity to get in a little exercise windsurfing, sailing, water-skiing, golfing or simply paddling about in a pedal-boat on the nearly always calm and warm Mediterranean waters.

Above, view of the Roquetas golf course.

Below, windsurfer.

View of the town of Roquetas de Mar.

It's not far to **Roquetas de Mar,** a town that identifies with the sea, as shown best by Roquetas' local festivals. On 29th December, while most of Spain is huddling around the stove ready to usher in the new year, Roquetas spends the day on the beach roasting fish in bonfires made of dried seaweed from the Mediterranean's own bosom. This is the old established festival of *Las Moragas.* And then in July, on the local feast day of Saint Anne, a maritime procession is held. The saint has her face washed in water from the port. The water is immediately returned to the sea in a clear token of the partnership between the saint and the sea at Roquetas. After that the saint's image is carried on board a lovingly decorated boat that casts off, followed by all the other boats sounding their horns, and so the seagoing procession begins.

Inside town you can visit the early seventeenth-century Castillo de Santa Ana, long abandoned but now recently restored, and the Iglesia de la Virgen del Rosario, a church dedicated to Roquetas' patron saint, which has a lovely coffered Mudéjar roof and decorative pictures at the main altar done in the sixties by the Almería artist Perceval. And you should also take a stroll through the fishing port to soak up the genuine Mediterranean seaport flavour. If you are out and about at dawn, you could attend one of the typical auctions of fish freshly pulled from the sea. The local fishermen consider the sea a female personage. And then a good *ponche pescador,* or "fisherman's punch" of white wine, liquor and a raw egg, well stirred, to drive out the cold. Does it ever work!

Previous two pages, aerial view of the Roquetas de Mar housing estate.

Roquetas de Mar. Castle and fishing port.

We'll wind up our tour of the coasts of western Almería at **Aguadulce,** which counts officially as a township of Roquetas. Old local fishermen say that the name Aguadulce, which means "fresh water," comes from springs of drinking water that used to well up right on the beach. Following up on the clue, the Institute of Colonisation conducted a little drilling here in the early 60's and the result couldn't have been better. There is underground water here, pure, plentiful melt-off from the Sierra Nevada. And so Aguadulce grew from a humble fishing village with 27 homes and 300 inhabitants at the beginning of the 60's to a big cosmopolitan city by the dawn of the twenty-first century.

If you visit during the summer you could attend some of the summer classes the university holds each year at the Hotel Playadulce, the area's pioneer establishment. The Urbanización Aguadulce, chronologically the province's first housing estate, was declared a *Tourist Interest Site* in 1966. Gardens abound at the Urbanización and all run down to the wonderful marina, which can accommodate 800 boats up to 25 metres long. The yearlong mild climate means that the constellation of pubs, restaurants and cocktail bars surrounding the Urbanización are open yearlong as well. Don't fret about where to leave the car if you drive in; there's parking space for 500. A wonderful place. Here's where we end our tour of western Almería.

Aerial view of Aguadulce.

Two views of Aguadulce.

Above, coastal hotel in the municipal district of Enix.

Below, the beach at Aguadulce.

Playa del Zapillo. Almería.

THE BEACHES OF THE CAPITAL

Before we reach the beaches of Almería we have to go through the municipal district of **Enix.** The district capital, the town of Enix proper, lies many kilometres inland and at a considerable altitude but the district does let the Mediterranean lap at its edge along *Playa de El Palmer,* a beach measuring a scant half-kilometre in length and hard to access because of a nearby tunnel.

The coast road practically hovers along the breathtaking cliffs of *El Cañarete* running right into **Almería.** It's hard for me to boil down everything you could see in my city into a few lines, so I'll just suggest four itineraries you could follow in Almería: The port, the Paseo Marítimo and the beaches; the Churches; the Old City and the Alcazaba; and the entertainment available along the "T" formed by the intersection of the city parks and La Rambla. We'll take a close look at the first itinerary as it falls in with our beach theme, and I'll just give you a rough sketch of the others, which focus on the city itself.

Port of Almería.

The Port, the Paseo Marítimo and the Beaches

Almería is known to have had a commercial port since the times of Abderraman III, who had a little shelter for watercraft built around 960 with its own lighthouse and all the conveniences. The 1522 earthquake, however, destroyed it. The port we see today was not built until 1847. It's a real treat to explore the port on a sunny winter morning or as evening falls in the heat of summer. Next to the port is the **fishing port** where at dawn every day Almería has the most original fish auction imaginable. From the port we go to the promenade, **Paseo Marítimo.** Almería has three kilometres of promenade. It starts at the old Cargadero de Mineral, an ore loading platform built in 1901 and disused since 1970. The Cargadero was recently declared an *official cultural asset* and is scheduled for an imminent facelift. Paseo Marítimo is all pedestrian. It takes us across a number of beaches that used to be separated but now segue smoothly into one another: *Las Almadrabillas, San Miguel, Villagarcía, Las Conchas, El Zapillo* and *El Palmeral.* You'll find a healthy population of pubs and sidewalk cafés strung along the promenade. In summer and at weekends the beaches are usually well-peopled but not really crowded.

Above, Almería at night.

Below, Maestro Padilla Auditorium.

Nowadays Paseo Marítimo comes to a halt at the Nueva Almería area of town. Along the last few metres of promenade you can see quite a number of sights: the fairgrounds that we dress up each year for our *Feria de Agosto,* a festival in honour of the Virgin of the Sea; multi-purpose sport facilities usually bustling with young people; and the Auditorio Maestro Padilla, an auditorium named for the famous Almería-born musician and composer and inaugurated by the queen in 1991. If you're in the area of a Saturday you can go shopping at the street market that springs up here weekly and stocks nearly everything including clothes, shoes, flowerpots, non-perishable foods and Morocco leather.

This wide avenue, Avenida Mediterránea, is one of the city's backbones; it runs straight through Almería. On it you can see the Pabellón de Deportes, a sport pavilion inaugurated in 1981 with the hotly-contested finals of the King's Cup Basketball Tournament between Real Madrid and Barcelona; the Frontón Andarax, a handball court built by the Handball Federation in 1988; the city sport facilities, always thronging with young athletes; a sweeping school ground; and, where the buildings begin to become sparser, a large shopping centre with over a hundred stores.

Two views of the port at Almería.

The Churches of Almería

We'll start our tour of the city's churches at **Puerta Purchena,** the heart of Almería, a square presided over by a handsome fountain and circled by lordly nineteenth-century buildings. It's a rule that you must drink a swallow of water from the stone pipe to fall under the traditional local prophesy: If you're single, you'll marry in Almería; if you're already married, you'll return. From the square we will follow a short itinerary that will introduce us to Almería's oldest churches. The closest is the **Iglesia de San Sebastián,** which began construction in 1673. Its main altar features a moving statue of Christ, *El Cristo del Amor.* Barely a hundred metres away is the **Iglesia de Santiago,** raised in 1559, which has a majestic tower. This church stands on a corner, and if you just turn down that same street you'll find the old *Aljibes Árabes,* cisterns built in 1038 by Zurhayr to provide drinking water for the Moslem population. And now you turn onto *Calle de las Tiendas,* the oldest street in Almería. It was opened in the eleventh century to connect the Alcazaba with the city gate. On this street is the **Iglesia de las Claras,** part of a thirteenth-century Clarissan monastery run by cloistered nuns.

◀ *Above, balconies look out over Puerta Purchena.
Below, close-up of details in the façade
of the Iglesia de Santiago.*

*Plaza de la Catedral (above)
and Renaissance porch.* ▶

And so we reach the **Cathedral.** Bishop Villalán
began building it in 1524. It has a Renaissance
façade but inside the décor is Baroque. There are
three naves and the central nave is bisected by
the choir. To the cathedral's right is the
Monasterio de las Puras, home to cloistered
nuns; it began construction in 1514. From here
we will set off down Calle del Cubo toward the
Plaza Virgen del Mar, dominated by the
Santuario de la Patrona de Almería. The
Santuario was begun in 1494 in a Gothic style
that was already very decadent back then. Its old
cloister now houses the Escuela de Artes. Going
up the street you'll reach the **Iglesia del Sagrado
Corazón,** built in the twelfth century but
completely restored in 1992; cloistered nuns
took charge of the church. We'll wind up our
tour in a leafy green square under the sober
Neoclassic **Iglesia de San Pedro,** right next to the
Paseo Marítimo.

◀ *Tabernacle at the main altar in Almería Cathedral.*

Plaza Vieja, Almería. ▶

The Alcazaba and the Old City

We'll start this route at the **Plaza Vieja,** the snuggest, quaintest little square in Almería. It used to host festivals, Christian markets, an Arab market and even bullfights. The main building here is the **Ayuntamiento,** an impressive Neoclassic town hall crowned by a clock that strikes the hours to the tune of "Fandanguillo de Álmería". Go under the arch to the right of the Ayuntamiento and that street will lead you up to the citadel that has become our city's symbol, the **Alcazaba.** It was probably built around the year 955, which is considered Almería's birthday. The Alcazaba's 43,000 square metres are split into three different sections. The first is covered with trees, gardens and fountains. A Gothic archway provides passage into the second section, the residential area where the Moslem governors used to live. And the third section is a castle tacked on by Ferdinand and Isabella when they took the city in 1489. It is a fantastic vantage point for looking out over Almería. From the Alcazaba we can walk down to **La Almedina.** In this neighbourhood is the Iglesia de San Juan, which was built on the foundations of what used to be the city's Arab mosque. We'll go down Calle de la Reina to the **Hospital Real,** a lovely two-storey Renaissance building, cloister included, founded in 1556. And we'll wind up our tour at **Paseo San Luis,** a cool park in the shade of a hundred-year-old grove.

Above, panoramic view from the Alcazaba.

Below, the Alcazaba, with Almería spread out at its feet.

The Alcazaba. The keep.

Parque Nicolás Salmerón, Almería.

Almería's "Entertainment T"

This "T" I keep talking about is made up of three great places for walking and window-shopping right in downtown Almería, the **Parque Nicolás Salmerón,** the **Parque de las Almadrabillas** and the **Rambla.** The Parque Nicolás Salmerón starts at the western entrance to the city, next to the port. This stretch of the park is known as the **Parque Viejo** or Old Park. A spectacular fountain carved of Macael marble, the *Fuente de los Peces,* marks the entrance to the **Parque Nuevo,** or New Park, full of gardens and pools. A bridge over the mouth of the old Rambla, a dry river bed, leads the way to the flamboyant Parque de las Almadrabillas, which finished development in the year 2000. To go inside you'll have to go under the old Cargadero de Mineral.

And on the horizon like a vivid stroke of watercolour stands the lighthouse, **El Faro.** Every lighthouse has a story. Solitary and remote but immersed in the social reality of Almería, though Almería rarely trudges the distance between to pay a visit. But the lighthouse is always looking out for the city, guiding it with that eternal wink. See you around, friend Faro. The crossbar of the "T" is La Rambla. The housing estate here took the entire decade of the 90's to complete. Quite the Pharaonic work of engineering and aesthetics, the Urbanización La Rambla wrought a definitive change on Almería's image. Divided into four stages, it starts at the edge of the city and ends of course at the sea.

The Fuente de los Peces in the Old Park.

◀ *The old ore loading platform.*

Below, Paseo de la Rambla.

THE BEACHES OF THE ALMERIAN LEVANTE

We reach the beaches along the Almerian Levante by the road through **El Zapillo,** the capital's tourist trap par excellence. We're following the Carretera de la Costa, as the road is known in Almería. We cross the bridge over the mouth of the Andarax River (or the Almería River, as it appears in the geography books), the only river in Spain that has gone absolutely dry by the time it reaches its mouth. After barely four kilometres we can spot the **university,** the prettiest campus in Spain if only because it's on a beachfront lot. Just a kilometre after that we cross through **Costacabana,** a charming, peaceful residential area with old-fashioned one-storey homes, each with its own garden. No, no duplexes here. In the meantime on the left we can view the runways, gardens and control tower of the **airport.** Opened in 1966 and enlarged 30 years later, the airport is now Almería's leading tourist gateway. And five kilometres down the road stands **Retamar,** another typical Mediterranean settlement with white houses and ample beaches.

Soon after that we'll see a little white and green sign announcing that we are approaching a truly special one-of-a-kind natural treasure, the **Cabo de Gata Natural Park.** Right after that you'll see a little sign on your right announcing that it is two kilometres to **Torregarcía.** If you follow the sign you will find a watchtower like the many others that dot the coast of Almería, and a little shrine. I wouldn't even have mentioned them if it weren't that they have a story attached. One cold morning of December 1502, the watchman in this tower, one Andrés de Jaén, saw something floating on the placid sea water. When he climbed down to see what it was he was awestruck to find that it was a beautiful dark carved figure of the Virgin Mary floating on the waves as if borne by them in procession to the shore. The figure was named the *Virgen del Mar* (Virgin of the Sea) and so Almería found its patron saint.

A shrine was built near the tower in 1951. The interior is decorated with a fine mosaic. It only opens its doors for the pilgrimage held the second Sunday of January. While most of Spain is trembling with cold we Almerians hold a nautical pilgrimage to bring the Virgin here and spend the whole day with Her.

Paseo Marítimo, promenading through El Zapillo with the tourists.

Torregarcía Shrine, in Cabo de Gata Natural Park. ▶

Stretch of coastline in front of the University of Almería. The Cabo de Gata is in the distance. ▶

Below, Torregarcía Watchtower, at the gates of the Natural Park.

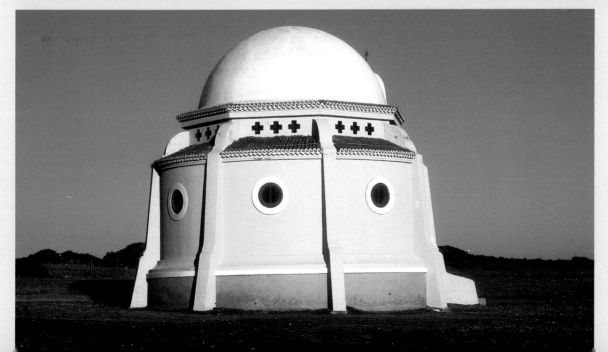

Salt mound.

Below, flamingos fish at Cabo de Gata.

Salt marshes at Cabo de Gata. ▶

Back on the road, we drive into the **natural park.** Created in 1987, Cabo de Gata was the first listed national park in Andalusia. It includes not only the landscape of fennel, bushes, reeds and eucalyptus you are looking at but also wide big ponds a few kilometres down the road where thousands of migratory birds such as flamingos, gulls, charadriiforms, avocets and black-winged stilts nest. And what's more the coast here is dotted with cliffs, sheltered coves, broad lonely beaches and even some reefs, such as the *Arrecife de las Sirenas.* Over more than 40 kilometres of road and 29,000 hectares of park you are going to have the opportunity to see an absolutely unique side of the Mediterranean.
As you go deeper and deeper in the park you'll notice the landscape begins to change. You'll go through the townships of **Pujaire, San Miguel, La Almadraba de Monteleva (La Fabriquilla)** and soon the road will begin to climb an enormous mountain wall that will threaten to stall your motor. This is the way up to the *Cabo de Gata lighthouse.* From there you can see fantastic views, scenes that you'd think were tricks if you saw them in a photograph. You can identify some of the beaches, coves and fantastic rock formations strung below you just from their names. There's the *Arrecife de las Sirenas,* or Mermaids' Reef; the *Arrecife del Dedo,* or Finger Reef; the *Playa de la Media Luna,* or Half-Moon Beach; and *Cala Raja,* or Slash Cove. At the foot of the lighthouse you'll also see a pretty mosaic depicting the local animal and plant life.

San Miguel, Cabo de Gata. ▶

A couple of kilometres later the going gets tougher, the asphalt runs out and a country road begins that isn't always fit for driving. It leads us past beaches, coves and small settlements. **Los Genoveses** is one such settlement, named for a group of Genovese immigrants who once built a little port on the site. The port is now gone. **Mónsul** is another, with sweeping dunes that shift back and forth as the sea eats its way inland. We're on asphalt again at **San José,** formerly a fishing village, now reborn as an ebullient tourist site with an elegant, lively marina that can accommodate 244 boats of a maximum depth of 4.5 metres.

Inland we find **El Pozo de los Frailes,** "The Well of the Friars", whose name seemingly comes from the two ridges that stand on constant watch over the well from their high vantage point, known popularly as "the Fat Friar" and "the Thin Friar". Continuing along this road we reach an intersection that will take us to three charming coastal villages. The first is **Los Escullos,** where nature's erosive power has carved out strange and wonderful shapes on the snowy sea cliffs near a restored seventeenth-century castle. The second is **Isleta del Moro,** an eye-pleasing arrangement of oases and sheltered coves. And the third is **Rodalquilar,** formerly a gold-mining town, abandoned in the 60's because it no longer turned a profit. It has now been outfitted as a campground for young people.

The Cabo de Gata lighthouse. ▶

◀ *Arrecife de las Sirenas, Cabo de Gata.*

Below, the beach at Cabo de Gata.

Cala de Mónsul.

Above, an aerial view of San José.

Below, the dunes at Mónsul.

Two views of La Isleta del Moro.

Cortijo del Fraile, the real-life scene of the story dramatized in Blood Wedding. ▶

Castillo de Rodalquilar.

Very close to here is the estate of **El Cortijo del Fraile,** the real-life scene of the story behind Granada-born poet and playwright Federico García Lorca's drama *Blood Wedding.* Here's the story, and it really happened: A woman named Paca Cañadas who lived at El Cortijo del Fraile was supposed to enter a marriage of convenience, as so many people did at the turn of the century. The night before her wedding to Casimiro Pérez, tragedy struck. Her true love, her own cousin Paco Montes, rode off with her on his horse along the very roads you are now travelling. But a brother of Casimiro's found out and lay in ambush for the lovers at a crossroad. He killed Paco in an attempt to remove the stain on his brother's honour. The romance mixes love and tragedy in a fitting setting of family hates, overwhelming passions and revenge.

After leaning out over the *Mirador de la Amatista* for the panoramic view, the coast road comes to an end at **Las Negras.** This village, population 300, huddles under a majestic, impressive black cliff that has repulsed all attempts to force the road through to **Aguamarga,** about 15 kilometres farther up the coast. But that distance can only be covered on foot or mountain bike. And that's a shame, because those 15 kilometres are the most spectacular bit of the park: Utterly virgin coves of amazing beauty, such as *Cala de San Pedro,* which has a spring fit to drink from and the remains of a Nasrid castle.

Las Negras.

Aguamarga.

Cala de San Pedro. ▶

Parque de Carboneras, with the castle at the rear.

The Beaches at Carboneras, Mojácar and Garrucha

After leaving behind the Cabo de Gata Natural Park, it's a good long drive out of sight of the sea before we reach **Carboneras,** reputed by its tourist bureau to be "the divine sea". The drive in is indeed gorgeous. Almost unexpectedly you're face to face with the Mediterranean again. There's a traffic island at the intersection with palm trees, rose bushes and geraniums surrounded by a green carpet of lawn, and there's another island out to sea like Neptune's sentinel posted there to keep watch over the town. The island looks close to the beach but looks are deceiving; it really lies 400 metres from the shore. Young people from the village commonly make bets on whether or not they can swim out to the island. And don't think it's such a snap, either. If I were you I wouldn't try, unless you are a consummate swimmer. By now you are seeing the fishing port built in the early nineties to satisfy a long-held desire of the local fisherfolk, because Carboneras has always been a fishing town. Carboneras has 16 kilometres of beaches, four of them inside town. There's *Los Cocones* where the port is, *El Ancón* in the middle of town, *Las Martinicas* heading toward the port area, and *El Algarrobico* on the road to Mojácar. Well, there is one more, Los Muertos, a nudist beach that can only be reached by sea or bike.

If you are in Carboneras you must go see the **Castillo de San Andrés,** a castle built in 1580 by the Marquis del Carpio to protect the area from a peculiar kind of smugglers, corsairs who used to raid coastal settlements for Christian captives to sell as slaves on the African coast. Naturally the locals eventually moved closer to the castle. A good time to visit Carboneras is 13th June because then you'll catch the feast day of Saint Anthony when the *Fiesta de Moros y Cristianos* re-enacts the erstwhile frequent attacks of Barbary pirates. The pirates mount a swashbuckling invasion from the sea in the morning and are thrown out of the castle as evening falls. The entire town participates in the show. And the best thing to do between rounds at midday is to get a table at one of the numerous local restaurants and order the fresh mouth-watering grilled fish, *parrillada de pescado.*

Aerial view of the coast near Carboneras. ▶

Above, Playa de los Muertos, in Carboneras.

Below, Playa del Algarrobico.

Playa de Granatilla, in Sopalmo. ▶

Above, Cala Bordonales.

Below, tower between Cala Bordonales and Torre Macenas.

Pueblo Indalo with night-time illumination.

The coast road rolls on between long sandy beaches and little by little it begins to rise toward the cliffs on its way to Mojácar. In these 16 kilometres of coast that separate the two villages we are only going to cross one township, **Sopalmo,** a charming oasis of palm trees, vegetation and jets of abundant water in the midst of mountainous deserts and dry river beds. And so we reach the long wide beaches of **Mojácar** with their superfine sand. Various housing estates are ranged along the beaches, all very white and respectful of the natural environment. There is **Pueblo Indalo,** the pioneer estate in this area, the Parador de Turismo and Marina de la Torre. They are all very lively and full of people, young folks in the summer and elderly patrons in the winter.

But for bewitching legend and mystery go to the village sprawling over the top of a nearby rise, Mojácar. Mojácar is the home of Almería's foremost symbol, the Indalo, a protective totem that keeps local residents safe from all kinds of curses including of course the feared evil eye. In the early 70's great streams of foreigners starting rushing in to get a first-hand eyeful of this thrilling hamlet where the women still covered their faces with a yellow veil and carried jars on their heads to fetch water at the nearby springs. Thirty years later the Indalo is still the icon of Almería.

No matter how hard you look though, nowadays you won't be seeing the old-fashioned brand of Mojácar woman, she who covered her face with a fine silk scarf but held no qualms about showing her legs in the public washing-places, the woman who used to slip the corner of her scarf under a jar on top of her head and pose her hands on her hips. Those women are gone forever. You can only find them in old engravings and pottery. But all you have to do is take a walk through the steep, tortuous, crooked white streets of Mojácar, where you never know where one street stops and another begins, eye-searing whitewashed walls dotted with many-coloured flowerpots overflowing with geraniums, grilles on the windows, shop-fronts and bazaars, streets that are just as likely to dwindle away under an archway as to run off onto an infinite stairway; all you have to do is wander through this Arab Andalusian labyrinth to find the spirit of those women.

◀ *Mojácar and the beach seen from the air.*

Quaint corners await in the town of Mojácar.

Monument to the fisherman, in Garrucha.

*Seagoing procession
of the Virgen del Carmen, Garrucha.* ▶

Let's leave the coast of Mojácar now and go on to the municipal district of **Garrucha,** another attractive seafaring town where you can still see the romantic dawn scene of the ships wallowing in from the high seas where they have spent all night fishing, full to bursting with the catch that will immediately be auctioned off at the fish market. The local tourist motto of *"Garrucha, sol y gambas"* is eloquent: Garrucha, Sun and Shrimp. The red Garrucha shrimp, you see, is a highly prized, extremely tasty item and Garrucha holds the Mediterranean red shrimp exclusive.

The prettiest place in Garrucha to take a relaxing walk is surely the wonderful Paseo Marítimo, which sports a lovely railing of white marble from Macael, a charming village in northern Almería province. Along the two kilometres of promenade there are three ports, the marina, the fishing port and the commercial port, one after another. And about halfway down the Paseo is the lordly Club de Mar. The entire scene is dotted with restaurants and pubs where you can try fish and shellfish fresh off the boat and cocktail bars that infuse the Paseo Marítimo with extraordinary youthful energy, especially in summer. Summer is also the season for the local festivals, held 16th July, with a bright traditional seagoing procession bearing the Virgen del Carmen. If you get the chance to be here, don't miss out.

Garrucha. Port and Paseo Marítimo.

Cuevas de Almanzora.

The Beaches at Vera, Cuevas de Almanzora and Pulpí

After leaving Garrucha the road turns inland for a time. We are in the municipal district of **Vera.** But very soon we'll be seeing the water again, at Vera's Urbanización Puerto Rey, the pioneer housing estate in this area. Bordering Puerto Rey we find the only naturist beach in the vicinity, *El Playazo,* which is inside the Vera Playa Club complex. And while we are gazing over the seemingly endless train of immense, fine-sand beaches, a sign informs us that we are driving parallel to Palomares in the district of **Cuevas de Almanzora.**

Palomares made headlines in half the world one far-off morning of 17th January 1966 when two US planes involved in a sky-borne refuelling manoeuvre crashed here. The alarm immediately went out. The four bombs they were carrying had sunk into the abyssal depths. All the world pored over the most detailed maps they could lay their hands on, trying to discover where and what Palomares was. Hundreds of US soldiers and experts swept the area with top-of-the-line detection equipment to avert catastrophe. Three of the bombs were quickly found but the fourth eluded all the technology aimed at it and remained in Neptune's embrace. In the end a local fisherman nagged the authorities into letting him take his boat out and he was the one who snagged the truant bomb using nothing more than his nets. From then on he was known throughout Spain as *Paco el de la bomba,* "Bomb-buster Paco".

Palomares. Church and Playa de Quitapellejos.

The road winds on along a chain of Eden-like beaches, reefs, a minor cliff or two, and most enticing of all the gorgeous coves, so sheltered, so solitary, so intimate. Each one has its own name. There is *Cala Cristal, Cala Mal Paso, el Calón, Cala Panizo* and, when we reach the municipal district of **Pulpí,** *Cala de los Nardos*. Let's stop here a minute because there's a lovely Marian legend attached to Cala de los Nardos, which means Spikenard Cove.

The spikenards that bloom there each spring have their mysterious explanation in a legend. One stormy winter night a fragile little boat lay helplessly adrift off these beaches. Its terrified crew screamed into the darkness, calling for help that they knew would never come because the sea was too rough and the coast too lonely and dangerous. Suddenly a miracle: The wind died down, a black thunderhead opened and let a faint ray of moonlight through. The fishermen could now see the coast and on it a woman dressed in white who signalled them with a lantern in defiance of the tempest. The crew finally managed to ground their little boat on the beach and fell to the sand exhausted by the superhuman effort. The next morning a delicious scent awoke the lucky sailors; the cove had filled with spikenards, perhaps planted by heavenly hands. If you visit this cove in the springtime you'll see just how true the legend is.

Port at Villaricos.

Beach at Villaricos.

Two view of San Juan de los Terreros.

And after driving through two lovely Cuevas de Almanzora townships, **Villaricos** (an old mining village) and **El Pozo del Esparto** (white houses and hard-working boats), we reach the eastern end of our Almería, the municipal district of **Pulpí.** Although the actual town of Pulpí lies nine kilometres inland, the district does have one foot in the Mediterranean, the township of San Juan de los Terreros. Terreros has always lived off the sea, but its recent discovery of tourism has enabled it to carry out an across-the-board modernisation of labour to handle all the visitors it receives, mostly in the summer.

Certainly the most striking thing about **San Juan de los Terreros** is its maze of coves and cliffs overhanging the sea. The *Cala de la Tía Antonia* is especially wild; it has quite a maze of caves, cavities and hollow rocks that writhe right along the seashore. And the wildest thing about them is that in the summer their lucky owners live there. They're the most fantastic housing estate of all, with their porches, doors and windows; some even have balconies complete with TV antennas. The rough path among these fairy-tale dwellings is irregular, now rising to the rooftops, now dipping nearly below the water, with unheard-of bends and angles. It's a real wonderland.

Cove in Sierra Almagrera, Cuevas de Almanzora.

Acantilados de Despeñaperros, the cliffs at Pulpí. ▶

Cala de Cocedores, Pulpí.

Pulpí. Isla Negra. ▶

Sunset off the Cabo de Gata.

Well, this is the end of our tour of the coast of Almería. If we were to go any father we'd be in Murcia. It's been 175 kilometres almost always within sight of the sea, and it has shown you, our friend and visitor, and me too what a gift it is for Almería to be bathed daily by the Mediterranean Sea.
See you soon.